LEGENDS FROM MEXICO & CENTRAL AMERICA

A QUETZALCÓATL

TALE OF CORN

Retold by Marilyn Parke and Sharon Panik
Illustrations by Lynn Castle

Consultants to the Series
R. Robert and Maria Elena Robbins

Fearon Teacher Aids
Simon & Schuster Supplementary Education Group

This book is dedicated to Katie, Todd, and Anna.

The illustrations in this book were created in Prisma Color.
The borders include renderings of glyphs from the Codices of Pre-Columbian
Mesoamerica (the region including Mexico and Central America).

Editorial Director: Virginia L. Murphy

Editors: Virginia Massey Bell and
Lisa Schwimmer

Cover and Inside
Illustration: Lynn Castle

Cover and Inside
Design: Marek/Janci Design

ISBN 0-86653-965-4

Printed in the United States of America
1.9 8 7 6 5 4 3 2

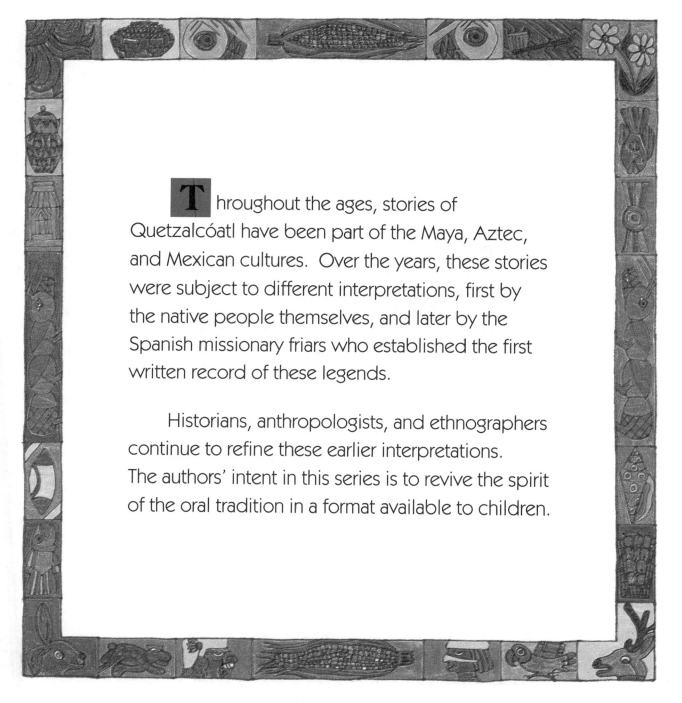

Throughout the ages, stories of Quetzalcóatl have been part of the Maya, Aztec, and Mexican cultures. Over the years, these stories were subject to different interpretations, first by the native people themselves, and later by the Spanish missionary friars who established the first written record of these legends.

Historians, anthropologists, and ethnographers continue to refine these earlier interpretations. The authors' intent in this series is to revive the spirit of the oral tradition in a format available to children.

Quetzalcóatl (ket-zal-CO-atl) is a mythological figure of the Mesoamerican people (the region including Mexico and Central America). He is considered to be kind and gentle and known for helping his people in time of need.

According to Mesoamerican legend, Tonacatépetl (tone-aw-caw-TEH-petl), or the Mountain of Sustenance, was the secret storage place of maize — or corn — the food of the gods.

Quetzalcóatl, the priest, gathered the children around the fire. He told them a story of the old, old days of his ancestor, Quetzalcóatl, the god. He told them first that Quetzalcóatl often took the form of a feathered serpent or bird-snake and that he once followed a trail of ants to Tonacatépetl, the Mountain of Sustenance, to find food for his people. This is the story that he told.

D icen que (they say that) long ago there was no food for the people of the earth.

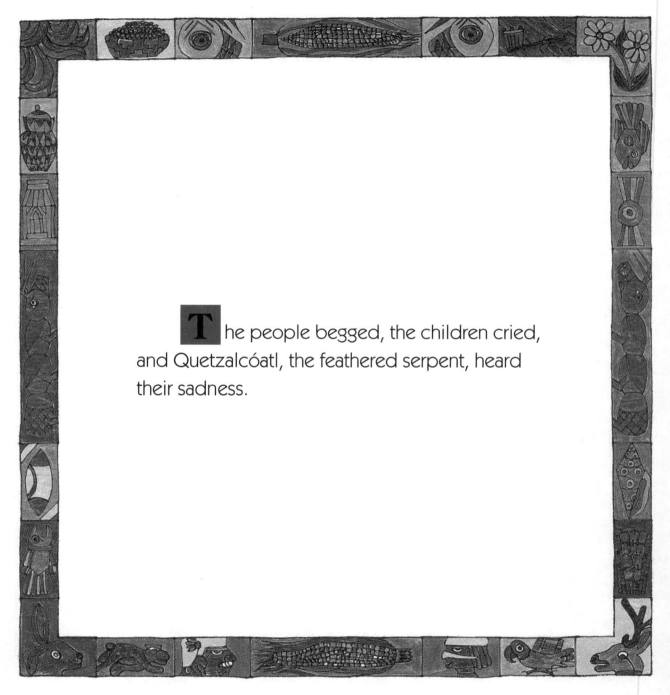

The people begged, the children cried, and Quetzalcóatl, the feathered serpent, heard their sadness.

9

Quetzalcóatl wanted very much to help the people that he loved.

One day Quetzalcóatl followed a trail of ants to Tonacatépetl, the Mountain of Sustenance, where the gods stored their food.

14

There he met an army of giant Red Ants who were standing guard over a spectacular array of corn.

Quetzalcóatl asked the ants for some kernels of corn, to which they replied, "Maize is food for the gods. Why do you want it?"

" **M** y people are hungry," said Quetzalcóatl.

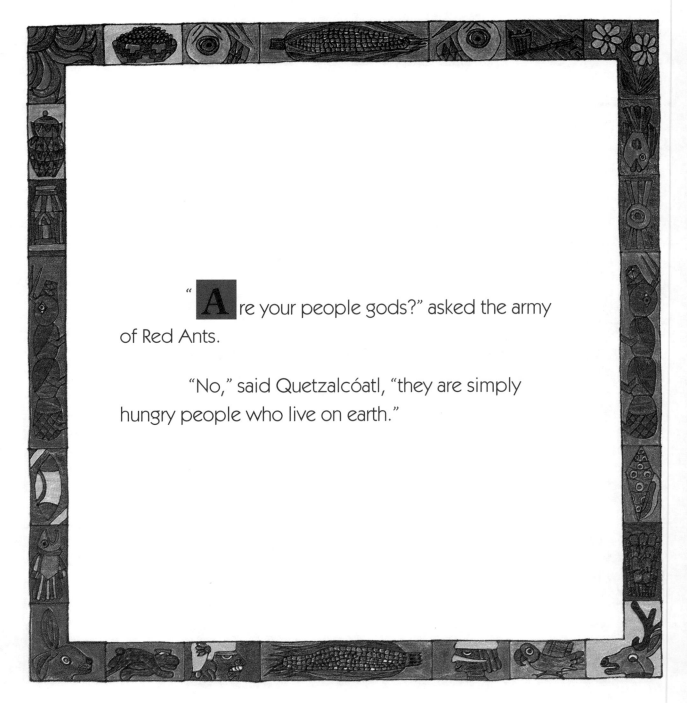

"**A**re your people gods?" asked the army of Red Ants.

"No," said Quetzalcóatl, "they are simply hungry people who live on earth."

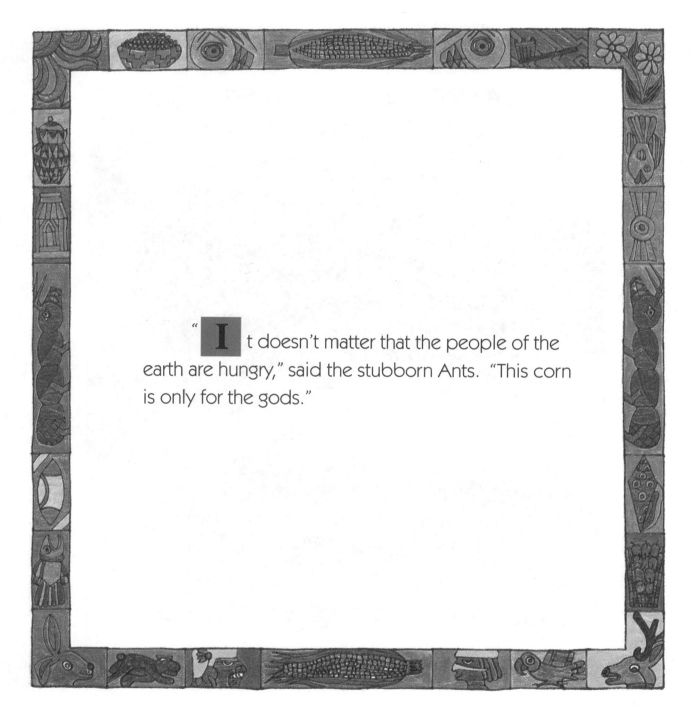

"It doesn't matter that the people of the earth are hungry," said the stubborn Ants. "This corn is only for the gods."

24

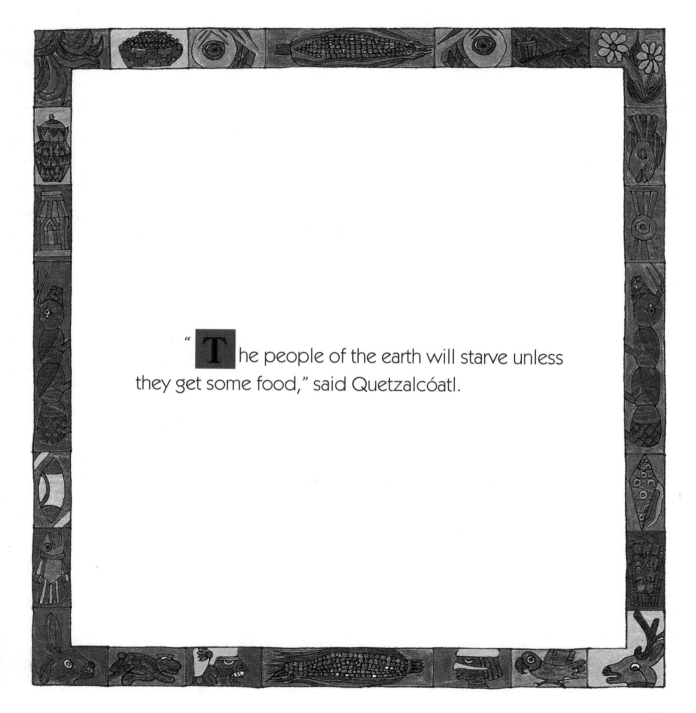

" The people of the earth will starve unless they get some food," said Quetzalcóatl.

"I must help my people," Quetzalcóatl said to himself.

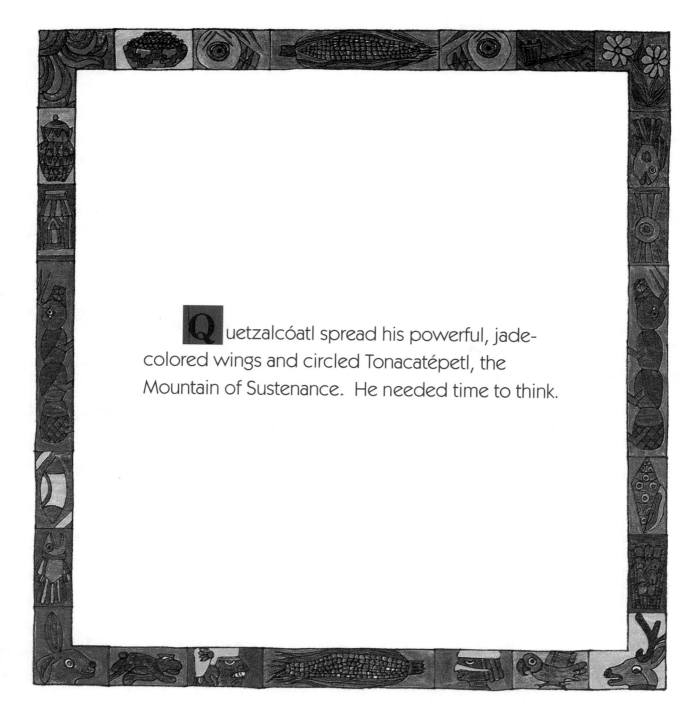

Quetzalcóatl spread his powerful, jade-colored wings and circled Tonacatépetl, the Mountain of Sustenance. He needed time to think.

"If I can turn myself into an ant," Quetzalcóatl thought, "I can take some of the corn back to the people of the earth."

31

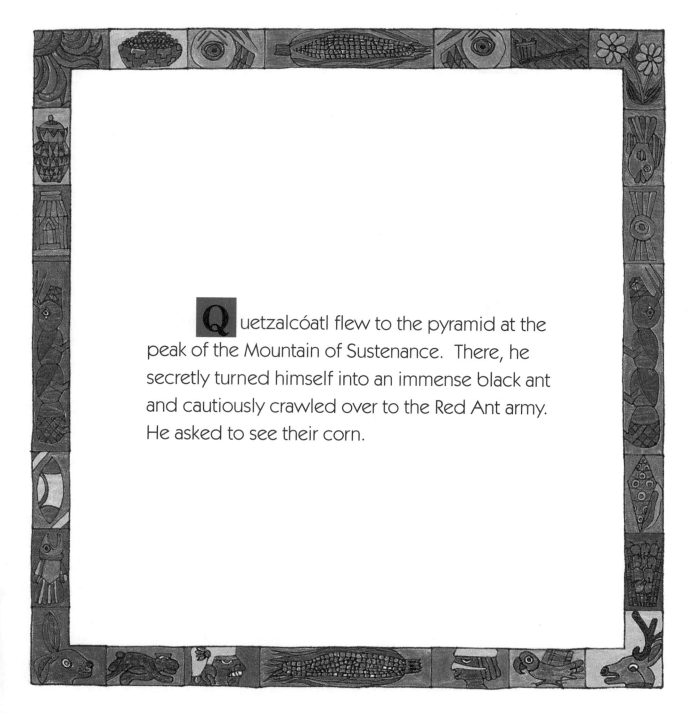

Quetzalcóatl flew to the pyramid at the peak of the Mountain of Sustenance. There, he secretly turned himself into an immense black ant and cautiously crawled over to the Red Ant army. He asked to see their corn.

The giant Red Ants were very proud of their treasure and eagerly took Quetzalcóatl-ant to the storeroom where they opened the enormous storeroom doors. There, Quetzalcóatl-ant saw corn of many colors — red, yellow, white, blue, purple, brown, orange, and black.

35

"**C**ould I hold some of this beautiful corn?" Quetzalcóatl-ant asked. "I would like to get a better look. I've never seen maize with so many lovely colors."

The giant Red Ants smiled proudly and handed Quetzalcóatl a kernel of each color.

With corn kernels in each hand, Quetzalcóatl-ant quickly turned himself back into the feathered serpent…

41

and swooped away with the precious corn.

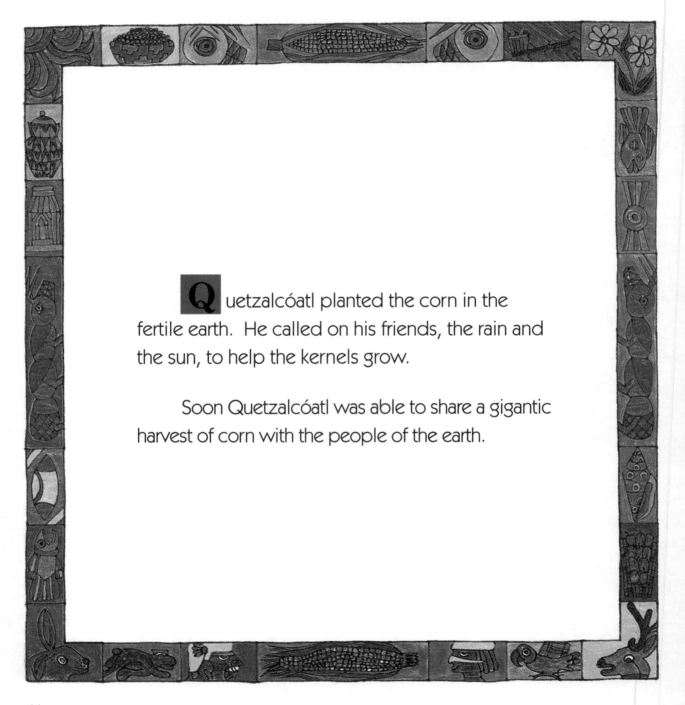

Quetzalcóatl planted the corn in the fertile earth. He called on his friends, the rain and the sun, to help the kernels grow.

Soon Quetzalcóatl was able to share a gigantic harvest of corn with the people of the earth.

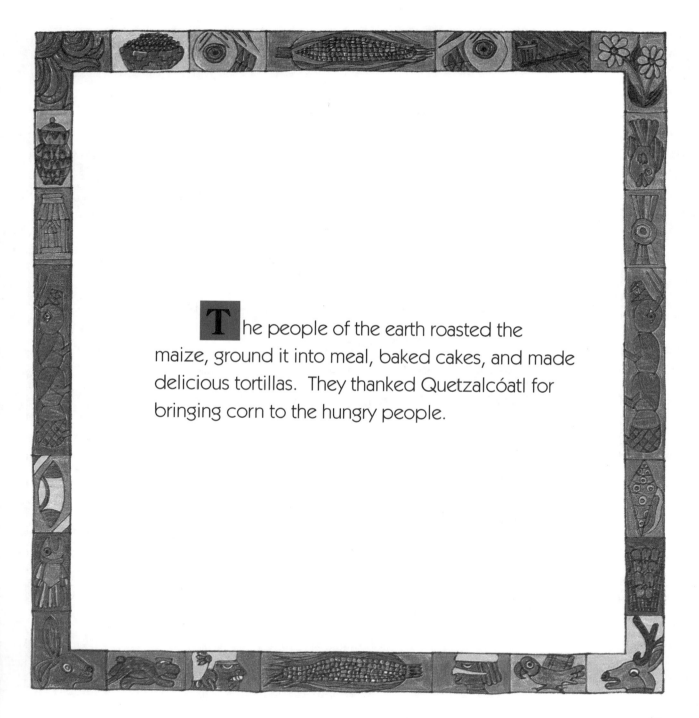

The people of the earth roasted the maize, ground it into meal, baked cakes, and made delicious tortillas. They thanked Quetzalcóatl for bringing corn to the hungry people.

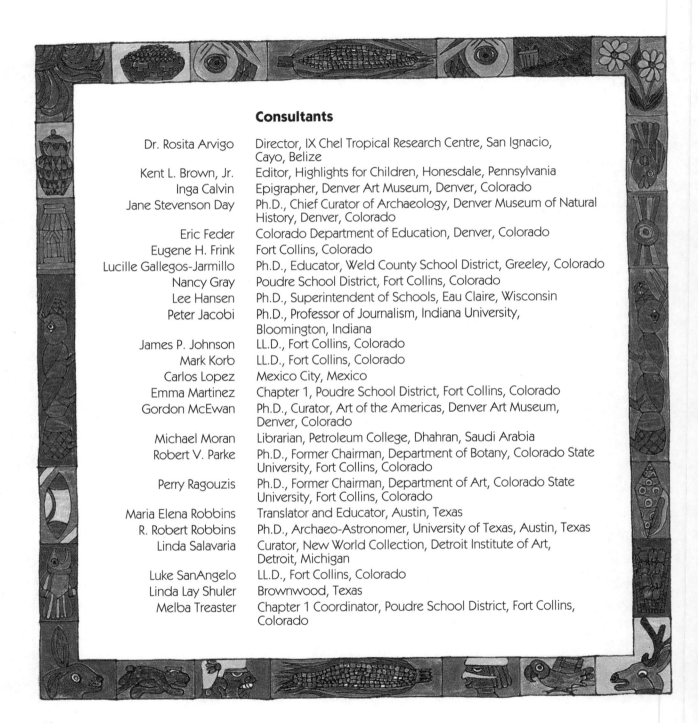

Consultants

Dr. Rosita Arvigo	Director, IX Chel Tropical Research Centre, San Ignacio, Cayo, Belize
Kent L. Brown, Jr.	Editor, Highlights for Children, Honesdale, Pennsylvania
Inga Calvin	Epigrapher, Denver Art Museum, Denver, Colorado
Jane Stevenson Day	Ph.D., Chief Curator of Archaeology, Denver Museum of Natural History, Denver, Colorado
Eric Feder	Colorado Department of Education, Denver, Colorado
Eugene H. Frink	Fort Collins, Colorado
Lucille Gallegos-Jarmillo	Ph.D., Educator, Weld County School District, Greeley, Colorado
Nancy Gray	Poudre School District, Fort Collins, Colorado
Lee Hansen	Ph.D., Superintendent of Schools, Eau Claire, Wisconsin
Peter Jacobi	Ph.D., Professor of Journalism, Indiana University, Bloomington, Indiana
James P. Johnson	LL.D., Fort Collins, Colorado
Mark Korb	LL.D., Fort Collins, Colorado
Carlos Lopez	Mexico City, Mexico
Emma Martinez	Chapter 1, Poudre School District, Fort Collins, Colorado
Gordon McEwan	Ph.D., Curator, Art of the Americas, Denver Art Museum, Denver, Colorado
Michael Moran	Librarian, Petroleum College, Dhahran, Saudi Arabia
Robert V. Parke	Ph.D., Former Chairman, Department of Botany, Colorado State University, Fort Collins, Colorado
Perry Ragouzis	Ph.D., Former Chairman, Department of Art, Colorado State University, Fort Collins, Colorado
Maria Elena Robbins	Translator and Educator, Austin, Texas
R. Robert Robbins	Ph.D., Archaeo-Astronomer, University of Texas, Austin, Texas
Linda Salavaria	Curator, New World Collection, Detroit Institute of Art, Detroit, Michigan
Luke SanAngelo	LL.D., Fort Collins, Colorado
Linda Lay Shuler	Brownwood, Texas
Melba Treaster	Chapter 1 Coordinator, Poudre School District, Fort Collins, Colorado